AMERICAN SAMPLER

Jane Duran

AMERICAN
SAMPLER

ENITHARMON PRESS

First published in 2014
by Enitharmon Press
10 Bury Place
London WC1A 2JL

Reprinted 2018

www.enitharmon.co.uk

Distributed in the UK by
Central Books
50 Freshwater Road
Chadwell Heath, RM8 1RX

Distributed in the USA and Canada
by Independent Publishers Group
814 North Franklin Street
Chicago, IL 60610, USA
www.ipgbooks.com

ISBN: 978-1-907587-38-2

British Library Cataloguing-in-Publication Data.
A catalogue record for this book is available
from the British Library.

Designed in Albertina by Libanus Press
and printed in England by
SRP

ACKNOWLEDGEMENTS

Warm thanks are due to Lynne Anderson, Professor of Education at the University of Oregon and Director of the Sampler Archive Project University of Delaware, who generously shared her knowledge and expertise on the history of samplers with me. My thanks also to Victoria Lochhead for her thoughtful advice on aspects of embroidery and samplers, and to Gigi Matthews for her helpful suggestions when I was researching this book. I am grateful to Allynne Lange, Curator of the Hudson River Maritime Museum; Linda Coombs, Program Director of the Aquinnah Cultural Center; Michael Dell'Orto and David Potter, Wilton Historical Society; Adam Nudd-Homeyer, Tappan Chairs; and Helen van Ham, Lyndeborough Historical Society, for their assistance. My warm thanks to Cheli Durán, Mimi Khalvati and Sue MacIntyre who read and commented on the poems with care and insight. All of these people have nourished this book.

The idea for my sequence 'American Sampler' was inspired by a beautiful sampler embroidered by Lavinia Dickerman of Hamden, Connecticut, aged ten, 1838. The poem 'Wind Map' makes reference to Theodor de Bry's map of Virginia, 1590. Hugh Brody's anthropological study of the Dunne-za, the Beaver Indians of Northwest Canada, *Maps and Dreams* (Faber and Faber, 1986) informed and inspired my poem 'To a Beaded Moccasin in a Museum'. The poem 'Letter from Stanley Abbot to Mattie Steele, January 29, 1863' refers to correspondence quoted in *From Schoolboy to Soldier* by Quincy S. Abbot (Abbot, 2013).

The Long Poem Magazine printed a version of my sequence 'The *Flying Horses* at Oak Bluffs'. The second poem in the sequence was suggested by Peter Simon's telephoto view of porches on New York Avenue in Oak Bluffs, Martha's Vineyard.

My heartfelt thanks as always to Stephen Stuart-Smith, my editor, and to Isabel Brittain and Peter Target at Enitharmon Press, for this sampler of poems.

In memory of my grandparents
David Henry Crompton and Lillian Crompton Tobey

You only learn *the* shape of the river; and you learn it with such absolute certainty that you can always steer by the shape that's *in your head,* and never mind the one that's before your eyes.

MARK TWAIN, *Life on the Mississippi*

CONTENTS

WIND MAP

The lines radiating from a wind rose
across an ocean or sail
help any ship to proceed with celerity

whereas a compass ponders another order;
however north is not always true north
and if the pilot eats garlic or onions

his breath can throw the lodestone
and needle awry, and where will the ship
and its mutinous sailors be then?

A patch of turquoise now appears
under the ship, signalling its whereabouts,
and the black loops and tangles of its riggings

billow. There is a definite coastline.
A woman with a water gourd,
some water splashing, and her naked girl

carrying a doll and rattle
come down to the shore
and from many points the wind beats in.

JOHN WHITE'S PAINTINGS OF THE NEW WORLD

Along with his demure watercolours
of milkweed and pursh,
his Portuguese man o' war

or the red grouper with its tidal stare,
soldier fish and lookdown fish,
blue-striped grunt and loggerhead turtle –

all he turned his hand to,
he painted the wife of the Timucuan
chief of Florida tattooed from forehead

to ankles, draped in blue Spanish moss,
carrying maize in her right hand
and a bowl of fruit in her left –

the fruit almost disappearing
in a turquoise haze,
everything that would seem

welcoming and hospitable and gentle.

TO A BEADED MOCCASIN IN A MUSEUM

I think of the dream a sleeper has
before the hunt – the real and imagined
trails he foresees, the marks he makes

on his dream-prey, his willed dream
moving unimpeded into the forest at night
to lead the way for him by day

when he will feel stones and twigs
and roots through the deer-hide;
and the tangle of tracks or impressions

made earlier by hunters in the forest
where no path lasts long, overlapping
and looping and cast wide, and gone

so the dreamer can see the animal and go to him.
But I am lost on the trail you still describe.

STONE WALL

The gaps in a stone wall make for shaky
errors of balance, yet embolden and hold

to show a trapezoid of pasture,
an hourglass of sky, a shark's tooth of brambles,

a black buffalo of pure shade. There is a fleck
in an otherwise perfect sky overhead

and no one here but me today.
I lay my palms on bird shit, lichen,

a borrowed rock, hefted and rolled
from a wild place, another carried, staggering

all the way from there to here
where the gaps steady and trespass.

NAMES

Stained from birth with Adam's sinful fact,
Thence I began to sin as soon as act…
                    Anne Bradstreet (1612–72)

Four girls are crossing a meadow
in their long-sleeved homespun dresses,
bearing down on the grasses
where the sun blows stiffly westwards.

The earth has give in it,
and the fractious horses bend down
to those deep drowned early morning grasses
they yank up so easily in their teeth

and chew in a circular, pensive motion.
Perhaps the girls will not mind
if I say their names quietly –
Electe, Submit, Silence, Humility –

just for the stories names tell,
or mention in passing their eager laughter
and strong, God-given steps
in the wet, greedy meadow.

THE RESIDENCE OF DAVID TWINING, 1787
BY EDWARD HICKS

A farmer in a dun coat holds the gate open:
all the black and white pigs, sheep, lambs and cows
are densely, dreamily packed together. One speckled bull
is elongated. A ram keeps patches of sunlight safe in his wool
and a woman reads the Bible to a boy under a tree.

In profile, a ploughman follows two horses
in a fenced field. The field is standing up on its side.
A rooster and goose cross the yard in tandem,
and a woman and man mount restless horses
with striped saddle blankets. There is a lot going on.

In the farmhouse doorway a black shadow keeps at bay
a young woman wearing a white cap and blue dress.
She is tiny – in proportion to the horse, colt, cow, calf
and girl carrying a bucket of feed and beckoning –
all existing in the third plane of the painting.

A barn, fences stave off what might be out there –
wolves or worse. There is so much to lose.
A haze of yellowy, unfelled trees beyond
are in the last – and only mysterious – plane.
Elsewhere nothing merges with anything else –

the ploughman, farmer, wife, child, bull, cow, sheep,
lamb, rooster, goose, calf, girl, horseman, dog, cat
are all created equal and religiously outlined,
placid and occupied, out and about in the open air
all the clement, live-long day that was.

PAPER BIRCH

I saw my chance – a strip of lined bark
peeling away, releasing the tree,

the bland, orangey or flesh-coloured
underbark already loose and fraying

but still damp and holding on somehow.
What scars did I leave on the living tree

when I tore off the rolled up bark
to write on? I thought it belonged to me,

or me to it. And anyway, what words
did I have then or now, or what stern

thoughts for so few words to wind round
each ream, ream, remember?

AMERICAN ELM

The national elm shadows run up a lawn
as far as a low, grey clapboard house
and back again in the heat, up and down
the small-paned, double-sash windows.

They have fled back and forth in this way
for over two centuries. The old panes
with their bubbles and clay particles,
ripple and bargain with the flow of elm leaves

as if their knowledge is questionable
whereas the new, replaced panes –
factory-made and absolutely smooth –
take up impressions and signals verbatim.

A caterpillar arches and stretches
to climb the bark, following its own lead
and resolution, up along and over
each bumpy and troublesome ridge,

and when I look into the past, wavy
banded glass breaks up each summons
and what I thought I saw
wherever the governing elm lingers.

TAPPAN CHAIR

Those who would live in this landscape
grow tall, deep, impervious too,

even laconic, splitting maple, turning white ash
on a lathe, stripping brown ash

from swampland, steaming, gouging,
pounding, bending, post, rung and slat

and all the time the wood so worked
makes a general, unpatterned noise,

a forest noise of force and flourishing
so the carpenter's heart beats faster

then stern and steady
in the making of a high-backed rocking chair.

UNDERGROUND RAILROAD

for Lois Ames, Sudbury, Massachusetts

Forgive me for telling this story
when you tell it so well – those cadences, pauses,
your intimacy with it, your white hair,
a descendant straight down the line.
You show us to our guest room
up the steep, wooden back stairs.

But first you stop by a deep fireplace.
No wonder you live here, hold to the house
and the house to you. Your grandfather
was a boy when he crept down those back stairs
and looked through the chinks in the panelling
and saw the firelight, black faces late at night,

runaways, gone in the early hours.
A tense stopping-station, the wagon hitched
to steal away to the next farm, all the way to Canada.
And the fireplace is still walk-in, pots and pans
blackened and hung. Your welcome to us
as I carry the suitcase up the stairs

in the oppression of an August night,
our little room at the top piled with books –
stories, poetry, journeys you take up,
inch by inch efforts you make now,
pain you feel constantly, the owl we listen for,
electric fan that lifts sweat from our faces.

It must have been winter then,
the faces wide-eyed in the firelight.
All night vertical blacknesses hold down farmland
and dew streams up in the morning, brash and blue,
up the screen door, broken breath of a horse
dragging the empty wagon home, stumbling whispers,

my boy on your doorstep, shucking corn in the sun
and you set the breakfast table, lay out
egg cups in your blue dressing gown, and we talk
and listen as old friends will and must,
and see a way, the many ways of telling it.

THE AMERICA

In 1852 James Bard sketches the *America*
from life and to scale and paints her in oils
in his studio so her banners and streamers

fore and aft fly out over the Hudson River
bringing pace and wind to the vessel,
her red paddlewheel rolling high

and raising a furor of trouble in the water.
The artist's clouds have birdlike shapes
and travel downwind, in the opposite direction

to the towboat, and a ray of smoke
from the stack pours out at a right angle
in sympathy with the errant bird-clouds.

A steam pipe also fires a slanting wisp.
This is the afterlife of the *America*,
pulling, in her aura of celebration

towards some greater momentum,
before breaking up at Perth Amboy, New Jersey
in 1896. Other boats to starboard

hurry along the brooding river
but they are far away and will not hide
the white, vigorous progress

of the *America* across the canvas.
For what she passes is incidental
to her refinement and downright

functionality – her red walking beam,
iron hogframe and towing bitt,
her paddlewheel with radial buckets.

A festive paddlebox keeps splashes in.
The male figures on her long port deck
wear black frockcoats and black hats.

Trees along the banks attend the spectacle
either from shadow or cheerful light,
but remain immovable, despite gusts

that blur the excited river, the waves
in the foreground more pronounced, darker,
(each carrying its own pale-blue brushstroke)

where I feel, I can't help feeling
the wind sharp on my face.

LETTER FROM STANLEY ABBOT TO MATTIE STEELE,
JANUARY 29, 1863

When you read a letter, a long letter
from someone you don't know
to someone you don't know –

a boy for instance, 21 years old,
in the Army of the Potomac,
to a girl in Portland, a bit older, say 23 –

perhaps his name is Stanley Abbot
and she is Cousin Mattie, say,
and he writes about the Mud March –

only four days in a long Civil War –
days of rain when the soldiers
waded for six miles through deep mud

and then had to corduroy causeways
to go all the way back to their original position
near Henry House, Virginia,

when you see his defeat and how he tries
to end the letter cheerfully, manfully,
for her – then you can imagine such mud,

mud that can't be dried by letters from home.
That's all it is, fathomless mud,
and he uses that word, *fathomless.*

Edward Stanley Abbot died at Gettysburg on July 8, 1863.

THE WAY WE LOOK AT YOU

photograph of an Apache resistance group by C. S. Fly, 1886

the way we stand and look at you
from scrubland, among thorns
and stones, not downcast

but looking straight at you
and the way a woman's hands rest
on her skirt, or a child squints

or Naiche's hands nearly touch
across his belt or the brambles
flare up behind us and in front of us

and our shadows join, but mostly
the way we look out at you
from a far place, from the wrong place

SMALL TOWN

… bounded as follows, beginning at a Spruce Tree
& Runs North by the Needle Two Thousand
One hundred & Ninety One perch
on province Land to a hemlock Tree Marked

The neo-classic public library at the top
of a steep lawn has an entrance portico
with four Corinthian columns. A woman
waits there with two hardback detective novels

then Runs East one Thousand five hundred
& fifty Eight perch on province Land
to a Township Adjoyning to & lying North
of the said Narragansett Town Number three

A river runs alongside the old woollen mill
and follows the road out of town
before going its own way, just a bit of it
showing its intentions, black and hopeful –
but rarely so since ice is taking hold now

then Runs South on said Township
Six hundred and forty perch to the Township
Granted to John Simpson and others

Once the forest lasted all the way to Canada.
In 1740, John Badger died of consumption.
His wife laid out breakfast for her children
and walked alone through the snow and woods
to the nearest settlers three miles away.
Her neighbours came back with her,
hollowed out a tree for a coffin

then Runs East on said Township
four hundred and two perch
to a Stake & Stones

Weak sunlight travels up and down
a disused railroad track.
When the track was new and silvery
the first wood-burning engine
whistled over it to celebrations in 1851

then Runs South One Thousand four hundred
and Sixty Seven perch on said Narragansett Town,
then Runs West four hundred & Eighty perch
on Duxbury School farm to a Stake and heap of Stones

A boy on a tricycle pedals fast down a hallway.
The wind travels across all boundaries
or falls open from the centre like a flower
as snow flurries begin, then thicken, burden
spruces, ashes, hemlocks, poplars,
stone walls, the well-lit houses on hills –
once the farms of early settlers

then Runs South thirteen perch on said Farm
to a poplar Tree marked, thence Runs West
One Thousand four hundred and Sixty perch
to the Spruce tree first named on province Land

Lines in italics are from a description of Salem-Canada, a tract of land granted by
the General Court of Massachusetts in 1736 to Salem soldiers or their descendants
who fought in the expedition to Canada in 1690. Parts of Salem-Canada were later
incorporated into the towns of Wilton, Lyndeborough and Temple in New Hampshire.

ICE HARVEST

Now that snow is touching the forest
in so many places
the men shovel out the rotting sawdust,

they lay down fresh sawdust in the icehouse
and wait for the ice on the pond to deepen.
They wait for the wind to turn dry.

Then they harness the horse, they load
an ice plough, chisels, hooks
and saws on a wagon and make their way

through the woods, as far as the glare –
a relief in the trees.

*

A woman in a long coat stands far away
on the ice, near the trees, in the sun
watching the horse and plough cut a grid.

She stands on her shadow.
She is precariously in the present.
Water slides out over the grid
and freezes immediately.

*

Sometimes if a cut is too deep
the ice can give way and a man
falls into the water, or a horse falls in
and is hauled out in commotion.

The woman curls her toes in her boots
and her fingers in her mittens.
The wind is porous and the voices
of the men are far away.

*

Somewhere in a forest
a pond is giving up
a little of its ice at a time
to the warming air that is ferrying,

moving the heavy ice
far and wide into the pine trees.

TADPOLES

I lay on my stomach and caught tadpoles
in my open hands so there was
everywhere for them to escape from.

The long shadow of the barn at the top
of the hill scrambled down
on all fours to the water.

The sun stayed up late.
Speckled tadpoles loosened over some mud
and weeds I barely touched

and swam off in all directions
though there was nowhere far to go.
Tonight there would be a lamp lit

in each room, my grandmother's hair
caught up in a bun, as she moved
from room to room, pulling the light with her,

and we would run and scatter over the wide
oak floorboards in our bare feet.

THE STRING

She is in a pond up to her knees
and a filmy mud is settling
around her ankles. That feels good.

I mean to ask her how she is
without disturbing her at her work
of tugging a sailboat in zigzags with a string.

She has wound the string round her wrist.
There is so much trust and commotion
in her gaze. The pond goes a long way out

and comes up for air somewhere curious
in the far pines. Perhaps everything I thought
I knew about her is mistaken. Her hectic shadow

in the water breaks in two at the waist.

MOUNT MONADNOCK

The only fault I find with old New Hampshire
Is that her mountains aren't quite high enough.
                                        Robert Frost

When we first met
how thin I was, all elbows
and knees, and you granite

and spruce, hemlock, bristling,
not soaring, sharing the same hours
and light with me.

Probably I was aware of you
in the corner of my eye – there,
reassuring, but no more than that.

Now you mean to be looked at
even at night, or from this faraway
time zone. When ice lays hold of you

and snow, I can crawl along your granite,
eye to eye with you, and feel fear
and a modest ambition.

Yet for me, dark or light,
these days it's all a matter of touch –
from your hand a single leaf

or even a pine needle would do.

AMERICAN SAMPLER
for Gigi Matthews

When I was grieving, the gold of our wheat field
found its way into my sampler and left flecks
of late summer. I embroidered the words
Nathan Snow was born February 12th 1804.
Nathan Snow died August 19th 1806.

I pulled each thread through the canvas,
each exhaustive emotion, near the window.
By then, stitch by stitch, burden by burden,
our clapboard house was complete
and a little apple tree beside it,

the greens staying strong in the thread.
A river might have run under the house
I embroidered. But I only stitch what is:
the wheat field that has not yet reached me,
his shadow that has not yet dawned.

A last bee comes to the windowsill, magnetic
and restful, released from the others,
and I loop and tug at a pale yellow knot
on the wrong side of the linen.

All the tiny cross-stitches make my sun,
my tree, my home, the turn of my wrist,
our hardships, surface and deepen.

Today the truth burned through.
I begin a blue alphabet high over the house.
Then I unravel the H, the winter doorway
before our pastures harden.

My aunt looks at my sampler, turning it over,
frowning now and then. Her moods or kindness
are there in my embroidery, and where I try
to please her makes itself felt in the conception.

Her own life draws out my meanings,
my fear of God in the prayer. Her hands are chapped,
well water has splashed her face.

My aunt's fingers barely touch the border
of wild strawberries by the house:
she will not smile, yet I know by the way she lingers
that she likes this best, and warms to me.

Wolves run through my sleep.
The mothers turn to me, blood and snow
round their mouths and stuck in their fur.
Howling, their cubs bring down drifts
from the hemlocks and into my eyes.

The wind loses them for hours. All night
is patient and drawn out looking for them.
Rows of singular fir trees glint.
My needle cross-stitches in out,
grey-blue numbers, the last a red 14.

Then daubs of blood in the snow.
1,2,3,4 … 14 wolves live on the mountain
in wilderness and family, the warm blood.

Stitching-time at last! Snow gives us
a closed-in time, these wooden rooms
and barriers. It is so deep in me, this snow.
I meet the drifts at eye level and back away –
the way I hold out and fold the washed bed-linen
with my sister, and the light in it lives on in me.

All the meadows, farmlands, bear a new weight
and persist. Under my woollen frock
my small breasts are growing.
Blue snow at dusk … and I count the stitches,
and I go out to meet them, crisscrossing the cloth.

Only one season is in my sampler: the known
or present, or the one I want to keep to
and continue long into the future;
the others gather behind it, or in front –
leader seasons that strew their plenty, scarcity,
and are my own flowering and fear.

Grasses come up through the snow again,
a low full moon, brush, bush, woods –
unpopulated, and at night the sense of snow
melting here and there, along our roof,
among the woodpiles, wherever there is black.

My mother climbs a hill and her skirt
billows backward. Early spring.
She calls to me and her voice carries far.
No neighbour for miles, but what is a mile
in this country? My voice also carries in the thread,
the honest thread I break with my teeth.

Or somewhere between the lines of my prayer,
am I there? My father ploughs our field
and each breakage shocks the earth
into repetitive furrows. Are these the only lines
I speak, as the ground churns and clots of earth
and fibre-roots fly up in resistance?

Or am I elsewhere, tangled in the wasted
threads, kept by me but never used?

Burial earth, cowshed, rooster on a roof,
a swarm of bees somewhere in the orchard,
thread by thread each destination is implicit,
glistening or giving out, yet going on …
a new thread or rescued thread in eyelet, stem,
queen-stitch. I imitate a fence, a moving tree.

Painstaking, I copy the alphabet, transforming.
Summer clouds overhead follow my stitches,
then also loosen and form God's letters.
Birds might appear as I embroider, but never do:
cardinals, orioles I live near, and listen for.
But I am obedient to the pattern I follow.

As I sew I hear a woodpecker at his bark.
He is not in my sampler, but is the way I sew
or place my border flowers, is even the letter
I am working on now, richer for that tapping,
for his held-away willow and echo?

Or are the deer running in the woods here too,
only because I think of them as I embroider
and my thought tightens the silk so it gleams
and has a tension I hadn't known before?
The air is moist and serene after rain.

My father combs the long flax, disentangling.
I think of my grandfather's beard, white and silky,
and how as a young man he took with his own hands
stones and boulders from the earth, combing
the earth through with his fingers.

Mist hangs over the open, soft, serious farmland
like a sermon I breathe. My mother settles
to spin the flax, wetting her fingers
so the fibres twist and cling.

So this coarse linen still has their touch in it,
where I touch and bleed and belong.

I trust in the woods that see me every day,
the mosses and their fine, thirsty silences
where a Pennacook mother once
carried her baby on her back.

Her feet tire in the forest ferns.
She goes over the brook and softly past
our well, into a clearing and our barn
bearing the weight of storm-clouds –
change, yet stillness.

And then she turns away with her sleeping baby
and this linen with my imaginings
borrows and restrains a course of light
shattering among the birch trees.

At night the lantern restores to relief
the flatnesses I sew, and widens the sampler
so it takes in faraway meadows,
mountain stories, lives beyond its scope.

The house flickers and bellies, retreats;
my apple tree billows, reminds, and the shadows
scatter and make real, deepen and enliven
here and beyond, drawing in the good scents
of wet pine and meadow, all-knowing,
consoling night, wavering and beckoning.

A sparrow passed just over my head,
barely brushing my hair, or raising a few hairs.
Someone will brush this sampler almost
with her fingers one day, to admire?
To recognise, girl to girl, how we are one
and the same? A timidity, but then a definite
caress and connection, flesh and blood, and I flinch.

*This sampler was wrought by Hannah Snow
aged 13 years 1807.* I cannot keep my needle still –
but must stitch and stitch, though the sparrow
is with me and distinct, its belly full of grasshopper,
its legs barely sustaining it, like futile thoughts.

And only a brown and rust glint in the birthdate
I am embroidering, near where the thread runs out,
and I take my sampler into the sunlight to find it.

My father is in the long drifts of hay, hauling.
Whenever I look, those bees are crossing
our pasture, fast, a continuous rush
from the wildflowers up to the hives.

At night my mother wanders through the house
with her lantern, to see us all asleep.
In her restlessness is she thinking of Nathan?
The walls flicker. My blue thread lasts for 40 stitches.

A sum of how many bees flies over the pasture?
I find my fault – a cross-stitch over three threads
and now the whole row is awry and slanting downward.

The forest is deep, there is no end to it:
hemlocks, maples, cedars, ashes,
deep as a twelvemonth, as the seasons
that take hold of me and let go one by one.

And the black bear's fur is deep,
his solitude – the rains come down on it,
the huntsman goes mad looking for it.

In my sampler everything lines up in rows –
alphabet, numbers, columbines, prayer,
the day my brother was born, the day he died.
But my canvas too is limitless and fierce.

When I turn my sampler over, the threads
confuse, though they still conjure pictures:
broken off threads tied into existing threads,
beginnings, all smoothed, taut and fastened,
but betraying frailty and repair.

Here my embroidered house is in the past,
my tree has its origins. Which side is true?
Yesterday a river bridge collapsed in the storm.
I can make out my lettering spelled backwards:
Mary Hutchinson was born January 4th 1773
Jacob Snow was born September 12th 1768
they were married April 14th 1792, part of a long
thought that continues after the words.

In candlelight my mother's forehead
and cheekbones gleam, also a line down
her long neck. Her hair is braided and coiled
and her eyes are lowered, though one eyelid
shines. She seems to be beginning some work
in her mind that knows no rest, as if now
she can pick up her thoughts and continue
to knit and unravel them. It helps her that night
makes such moments simple for her,
she can take them and roughen them
and nothing shows of her travails. Any agony
she feels serves to give her repose
since in the day all her face shines forth.

My brother is caught in this rescue-weave.
For him the threads tighten and the boundaries
keep. The joins won't show – held in place firmly.

Something to touch – a spelling that binds warp
to weft. *Nathan Snow,* grave and sweet,
turns back as if this sampler were heavy pages
and his own pages uncut still. And he searches

in my hands, my threads, here on this linen
for his earth and time, for a place to be
near this house, this fence, this tree.

NEW HAMPSHIRE SHADE
for Mimi Khalvati

There is a depth to this shade
I know nowhere else – it borrows its tone
from the rust clapboard house it clings to,

a red barn it splays out from,
from thoughts of empty streets
in a small town, early afternoon.

Shade I can rest in whenever I want:
a reminder – like a bookmark,
or simple geometry – a child could figure it –

the angle of sunlight and eaves
drawn with a gigantic protractor.
The cows grazing in the far meadow

are insubstantial in this heat, mere outlines –
sometimes even the outlines broken.
A woodpecker clings to the willow

and excavates, his red crest flung back
in an attitude of questioning or hectoring.
But the shade I find in familiar places

where I no longer belong
is no more than bearable thirst
and no rain yet.

LATE SUMMER, NEW HAMPSHIRE

A breeze is working its way
through the cornfield.
Where are the deep pathways out?

All night there is a plaintive
lowing whenever wind
and rain advance in the dark,

hesitant, as if learning each step,
and by morning the river is higher
as it passes an abandoned mill

and drenched, shining porches,
and dogs tumble their way
down steep, narrow stairs.

SAILOR'S WOOLIE

By then the rigging barely held, basted
with loosened, sagging brown cotton threads
but the sails were still tight-packed,

woollen cream chain-stitches, stiffened for travel,
all pressed to a sky that was mainly cloud –
long, straight lines of yellowing crewel

in a shattered arc around the ship.
In its sturdy mahogany frame
the ship had such a raw memory of its heyday!

My grandmother hung it on the wainscot
over the fireplace, where inland light
from the open sash windows could easily find

and fade it. The pineboard backing had a knothole,
so the lowest patch of cloud, near the hull,
was spotted with mildew or insect life.

That fierce hull with its 39 gun ports
and separate British and English flags
rested on dense, impenetrable blue-black water –

yarn over yarn, a sailor's touch and patience
that would hold it up or sink it.

*Sailors' woolies (woolworks) are embroideries made mainly by British sailors
in the 19th century, with portraits of their ships.*

CAPTAIN TURNER

Captain Turner once fished for swordfish and lobsters
and maybe he hankers after that life.
Or maybe he's relieved. Was he more alive then

when he turned his jaw to those winds, or now
as he carves seagulls from balsam in the harbour
and stands them on driftwood, each, each, each?

The sea passes below my feet in deep, muscly currents,
and I look over at a little island, breathlessly near,
no longer than a fishing smack, where seagulls land

in the grasses. Sometimes they stand very still
for long periods and the wind blows their feathers
about mercilessly. Captain Turner's driftwood

has experienced all manner of waves and weather.
His seagulls all look rather similar – their wings
are folded calmly, though one of his carvings

has the alert aspect of a gull about to stir.
But when I sit on my rock and eat my ice cream
slowly, chocolate through and through,

the long grasses and seagulls on the little island
glow and shiver with a restless life.

THE *FLYING HORSES* AT OAK BLUFFS
for Michael and Audrey Straight

The horses run counterclockwise
on this carousel in a wooden town,
all the ornamental afternoon.

What signals should I trust?
The piped organ music, the brass ring?
Or when a boy in line kicks one heel up

suddenly behind him, smartish,
in eagerness and impatience?

*

I look down through the porches
on the avenue, slatted rocking chairs
and hanging flowers,

a woman in a dressing gown, feet up,
ferns that separate the houses,
everything fernlike, filtered, cast off

or peeling, a study in how to intercept
light with dowels, posts and pillars.
As if repose or a limitless certainty

were pulled through to the last porch,
and the woman in the rocking chair
is receptive, passive and real.

*

Where is the girl so beautiful and dark,
who sang on the swing in the barn,
who transfixed our fathers?

She sings *blow the candles out,*
her bare feet touch the splintery floor.
And in the open barn window

downpour leaves, helpless in the rain.
We don't know much yet,
gathering in the barn to listen,

and we speak out of fear or weather
or respect, courteously to our elders.

*

My mother is scaling fish at the sink.
Scales on her hands, a rim of them
on her wrist. Drifts of rain

enter the kitchen window.
It is easy to be distracted here.
Rain keeps close to the shingles

leaning its whole weight against the house.
The effort to withstand
is what the house has come to.

And the rain, not knowing
how to get free of the house, speaks
to the interior, its soft mouth to the outer wall.

*

The shade behind a red barn
drinks the sun to the dregs.
All of daylight is in it.

The shade is nearly black
but green is hiding away in it.
Barn that swoops and swaggers

over the intense life of a hill.
Even my voice is deeper, milder,
more patient here.

The rope-swing in the doorway
lifts me into clean, open air
over the farmlands

and horses – gradually
slow, slower.

*

There are no shallows anywhere –
all depth, all black depth
wherever you enter from

(our side has a little pier) and almost a mile
out to the raft – you can just see it
like a stubby pencil line on the water.

Our arms are strangely caught and freed,
perfectly clear in that black water, yellowy,
caught by it. Our childish hands –

that sallow clarity we stay steady for.

*

The girls lie down in the clay pool
under the cliff, till they are old,
worn, aggrieved, covered with fissures,

the blue-grey touching each lock, caked.
Then they all stand up like the early world
and wave and shout to their families

below – dogs and ocean rotating,
the grip of seaweed
bound for elsewhere and captivated.

*

My orange horse is wounded,
backed into shade, backed into lustre.
But here everything heals quickly

and harshly. These carousel horses
don't go up and down
yet the landscape we pass

changes and allures
and on the turn struggles
to repeat each trying detail.

The horses blur, turning fast,
all the trials of my days are one,
any certainty I had tentative now,

gathered up but then fleeing.
A kindness, galloping, brisk and green.

*

Of the orange horse whose neck shines;
the russet horse who follows
a glowing somewhere out at sea

or in his oxide eye. Of the tawny horse
who knows where to go
and rushes at it – a glimpse of storm,

then leaps. Of the mustard horse:
whatever struggles he made, circling,
have brought him to his own darkness.

Of the brown mare with red nostrils
and a pale blue saddle blanket.
She leans backwards slightly, one hoof raised,

a tiny carved animal in her gazing eye.

CAPE PORPOISE
for Dorothy

Are those the same islands
we saw, or just rocks

or the tones of rocks
where no one can tread?

Even the outermost dot
is a thought blown so far out

now it is almost gone.
What happened between us?

Perhaps nothing – each imagined
a fault and a hurt, a jagged hurt.

Or maybe there was no hurt, just
a mistaken impression and years

of silence in a believable landscape
where everything and everywhere

is just as it always was.

AQUINNAH

For we are the people of the first light.
        Ramona Peters, Wampanoag

Because the light is so intense
I cannot see far enough into it

to find what is there − or who −
just the people closest to me

around a picnic table on a hill,
near the tribal farmhouse-museum

with Wampanoag artefacts,
necklaces, arrowheads.

Even the Atlantic is concealed,
and Nomans Land across the water −

munitions burial-ground, reserve
to oystercatchers, plovers, harriers

and seals that wash up entangled
in blue plastic fishing nets.

It's our last day on the island.
Reflections, ritual crossings, births

and dissolutions, and the tones of our voices
lilt, merge. The experiences of others

drift through me. The same light
everywhere I look, the same invisibles.

THE BASKETBALL COURT IN CENTRAL PARK

At once my boy slid off the bench and ran
to the far hoop. Now I could watch,
I could be there, it was summer

and the light would not go for a long time.
I thought of my own childhood in Manhattan,
even the metal roller skates

I used to strap to my shoes –
an assortment of partial, benign images
in a vector I was too peaceful to see beyond

all leading to this bench in Central Park.
When dusk came in the older players
wandered off – their game, the leaping

and shouts had been wholesome and friendly.
My boy took a last shot at the basket –
he did a layup with his left hand

and the ball held still in the air – it stopped
just higher than the hoop, slightly
to one side, and stayed there permanently.